Duncan Hines

Celebrates BAKING

BEEKMAN HOUSE

Library of Congress Catalog Card Number: 90-

ISBN: 0-517-03593-6

This edition published by Beekman House, Distributed by Outlet Book Company, Inc., a Random House Company, 225 Park Avenue South, New York, New York 10003.

Pictured on the front cover: Orange No-Bake Cheesecake (*page 14*), Double Nut Chocolate Chip Cookies (*page 28*), Carrot Cake (*page 9*) and Chocolate Cherry Cake (*page 71*).

Printed and bound in Yugoslavia
8 7 6 5 4 3 2 1

Duncan Hines

Come celebrate baking with Duncan Hines. Offered here are more than 80 versatile recipes to help you bake your best. Our staff of home economists in the Duncan Hines Kitchens have created these recipes to meet your busy lifestyle. Whether you're looking for a super-quick family dessert for a mid-week dinner, or a special cake for that PTA or church bake sale, you're sure to find the perfect dessert here.

Each of these recipes has been specially formulated for use with Duncan Hines cake mixes. And you can bake them with confidence because all the recipes have been tested and tasted by my staff of professional home economists in our kitchens. And to help you bake your best, we've added informative baking tips throughout — you'll find one at the end of each recipe. So from our kitchen to yours, good baking!

Pam Fry
The Duncan Hines Kitchens

From left to right in the Duncan Hines Kitchens: Lois Varland, Bobby Dempwolf, Debbie Vargo,
Pam Fry and Marilyn Munnecke.

When you need recipe help, call the Duncan Hines Kitchen Connection. Whether you have questions about these recipes, or about any of our products, help is just a toll-free phone call away. Let Duncan Hines help you bake your best. Call us at 1-800-DH MOIST, Monday through Friday, 9 am to 5 pm eastern standard time.

Gwenn Hawk Brima
The Duncan Hines Kitchen Connection

Our Kitchen Connection Staff. Front row, from left to right: Doris, Linda, Jenny and Tracey. Back row, from left to right: Mary, Geri, Wanda, Gwenn, Joan, Becky and Donna.

Twin Angel Food Party Pies

12 to 16 servings

1 package Duncan Hines® Angel Food
  Cake Mix

FILLING

2 packages (4-serving size) chocolate
  instant pudding and pie filling mix
3 cups milk
½ teaspoon almond extract

1 container (16 ounces) frozen non-dairy
  whipped topping, thawed and
  divided
1 can (21 ounces) cherry pie filling

1. Preheat oven to 375°F.

2. Prepare, bake and cool cake following package directions.

3. Cut cake in half horizontally with serrated knife. Place on serving plates with cut sides up. Cut around cake 1½-inches from outer edge, down ¾-inch and through to center. Gently pull out cut cake to leave a 1½-inch wide rim. Fill center hole with removed cake. Repeat for second half.

4. **For filling**, combine both packages of pudding mix in large bowl. Prepare following package directions, using 3 cups milk and ½ teaspoon almond extract. Fold in 2 cups whipped topping.

5. Fill each cake with half the pudding mixture. Spoon half the cherry pie filling around outer edge of each cake. Garnish each cake with dollops of whipped topping. Refrigerate until ready to serve. To serve, cut filled cake as you would a pie.

■ *Tip: Try different flavor combinations of instant pudding and pie filling such as vanilla instant pudding and pie filling mix and blueberry pie filling.*

Twin Angel Food Party Pie

Carrot Cake

CAKE

1 package Duncan Hines® Moist Deluxe
   Yellow Cake Mix
2 cups grated fresh carrots
1 can (8 ounces) crushed pineapple,
   undrained

½ cup water
3 eggs
½ cup Crisco® Oil or Puritan® Oil
½ cup finely chopped pecans
2 teaspoons cinnamon

FROSTING

2 packages (3 ounces each) cream
   cheese, softened
⅓ cup butter or margarine, softened

1½ teaspoons vanilla extract
3½ cups confectioners sugar
1 teaspoon milk

1. Preheat oven to 350°F. Grease and flour 13×9×2-inch pan.

2. **For cake**, combine cake mix, carrots, pineapple, water, eggs, oil, pecans and cinnamon in large bowl. Beat at low speed with electric mixer until moistened. Beat at medium speed for 2 minutes. Pour batter into pan. Bake at 350°F for 35 to 40 minutes or until toothpick inserted in center comes out clean. Cool in pan.

3. **For frosting**, combine cream cheese, butter and vanilla extract in large bowl. Beat at medium speed with electric mixer until smooth. Gradually add confectioners sugar and milk, mixing well. Spread on cooled cake. Refrigerate until ready to serve.

■ *Tip: Score cake into serving pieces and garnish with pineapple tidbits and pecan halves.*

Cherry Angel Delight

1 package Duncan Hines® Angel Food
   Cake Mix
2 envelopes whipped topping mix
1 package (8 ounces) cream cheese,
   softened and cut in small pieces

1⅓ cups confectioners sugar
1 can (21 ounces) cherry pie filling

1. Preheat oven to 375°F.

2. Prepare, bake and cool cake following package directions.

3. Prepare topping mix following package directions. Add cream cheese. Beat until smooth. Add confectioners sugar. Mix until blended.

4. Trim crust from cake. Cut into bite-size pieces. Place half the cake pieces in a 13×9×2-inch pan. Cover with half the cheese mixture. Repeat with remaining cake. Cover with remaining cheese mixture. Refrigerate several hours or overnight.

5. Spread pie filling over top of dessert. Refrigerate until ready to serve.

■ *Tip: If you're trying to cut down on calories, use reduced-calorie cream cheese and pie filling.*

Carrot Cake

Fudge Marble Pound Cakes

36 slices

1 package Duncan Hines® Moist Deluxe
   Fudge Marble Cake Mix
1 package (4-serving size) vanilla instant
   pudding and pie filling mix

4 eggs
1 cup water
⅓ cup Crisco® Oil or Puritan® Oil

1. Preheat oven to 350°F. Grease and flour two 9×5×3-inch loaf pans.

2. Set aside cocoa packet. Combine cake mix, pudding mix, eggs, water and oil in large bowl. Beat at medium speed with electric mixer for 2 minutes. Measure 1 cup batter. Place in small bowl. Stir in cocoa packet.

3. Spoon half the yellow batter in each loaf pan. Spoon half the chocolate batter on top of yellow batter in each pan. Run knife through batters to marble. Bake at 350°F for 45 to 50 minutes or until toothpick inserted in center comes out clean. Cool in pans 5 minutes. Carefully loosen cakes from pans. Invert onto cooling rack. Cool completely. Cut loaves in ½-inch slices.

■ *Tip: To make fudge marble ice cream sandwiches, cut ½ gallon brick of fudge marble ice cream into ½-inch slices. Put ice cream slices between slices of pound cake.*

Lemon Cooler

12 servings

1 package Duncan Hines® Moist Deluxe
   Lemon Supreme Cake Mix
½ cup butter or margarine, melted
1 package (8-serving size) lemon gelatin
1 package (4-serving size) lemon gelatin
3 cups boiling water

⅓ cup lemon juice
2 teaspoons grated lemon peel
1 quart vanilla ice cream
   Whipped cream and additional grated
   lemon peel, for garnish

1. Preheat oven to 350°F. Grease and flour 13×9×2-inch pan.

2. Combine cake mix and melted butter in large bowl. Beat on low speed with electric mixer until crumbs form. Spread in pan. Bake at 350°F for 20 minutes. Cool completely.

3. Combine both gelatin packages and boiling water in large bowl. Stir until gelatin is dissolved. Add lemon juice and peel. Stir. Spoon ice cream into hot gelatin mixture. Stir until ice cream melts. Refrigerate until mixture starts to thicken. Pour over cooled crust. Refrigerate until firm.

4. Cut into 3×3-inch squares. Serve topped with whipped cream sprinkled with grated lemon peel, if desired.

■ *Tip: You can use other fruit flavored gelatins in place of lemon.*

Fudge Marble Pound Cake

Praline Topped Cake

12 to 16 servings

1 package Duncan Hines® Moist Deluxe
  Butter Recipe Golden Cake Mix

TOPPING

⅔ cup firmly packed brown sugar
¼ cup butter or margarine, softened

2 tablespoons milk
1 cup finely chopped pecans

1. Preheat oven to 375°F. Grease and flour 13×9×2-inch pan.

2. Prepare and bake cake following package directions.

3. **For topping**, combine brown sugar, butter and milk in small bowl. Mix thoroughly. Stir in pecans. Spread mixture over warm cake. Broil 5 inches from heat 2 or 3 minutes or until topping bubbles. Serve warm.

■ *Tip: A good cake to bring to picnics or pot-luck dinners because you serve it directly from the pan.*

Pineapple Orange Pound Cake

12 to 16 servings

CAKE

1 package Duncan Hines® Moist Deluxe
  Pineapple Supreme Cake Mix
1 package (4-serving size) vanilla instant
  pudding and pie filling mix

4 eggs
1 cup Citrus Hill® Orange Juice
⅓ cup Crisco® Oil or Puritan® Oil
1 tablespoon grated orange peel

GLAZE

⅓ cup sugar

4 tablespoons Citrus Hill® Orange Juice

1. Preheat oven to 350°F. Grease and flour 10-inch Bundt® pan.

2. **For cake**, combine cake mix, pudding mix, eggs, 1 cup orange juice, oil and peel in large bowl. Beat at medium speed with electric mixer for 2 minutes. Pour into pan. Bake at 350°F for 50 to 60 minutes or until toothpick inserted in center comes out clean. Cool 25 minutes in pan. Invert onto serving plate.

3. **For glaze**, combine sugar and 4 tablespoons orange juice in small saucepan. Simmer 3 minutes. Brush warm glaze on cake.

■ *Tip: Serve with peach ice cream.*

Praline Topped Cake

Orange No-Bake Cheesecake

12 to 16 servings

CRUST

1 package Duncan Hines® Moist Deluxe Pineapple Supreme Cake Mix

½ cup butter or margarine, melted

FILLING

1 package (4-serving size) orange gelatin
1 cup boiling water
2 teaspoons grated orange peel
2 packages (8 ounces each) cream cheese, softened

1 cup whipping cream
½ cup dairy sour cream
1 can (11 ounces) Mandarin orange segments, drained

1. Preheat oven to 350°F.

2. **For crust**, combine cake mix and melted butter in large bowl. Mix at low speed with electric mixer until crumbs form. Pour into 9-inch springform pan. Lightly press crumbs 1 inch up sides. Smooth remaining crumbs out in bottom of pan. Bake at 350°F for 20 minutes. Cool.

3. **For filling**, dissolve gelatin in boiling water in small bowl. Add orange peel. Refrigerate until mixture begins to thicken.

4. Beat cream cheese until smooth in large bowl. Gradually beat in gelatin.

5. Beat whipping cream until stiff in small bowl. Fold into orange cream cheese mixture. Pour into cooled crust. Refrigerate until firm, about 3 hours.

6. Drop teaspoonfuls of sour cream around edge of cheesecake. Garnish with drained orange segments.

■ *Tip: You can use other fruit flavored gelatin in place of orange. Garnish with appropriate fruit.*

Coconut Crunch Cakes

16 servings

1 package Duncan Hines® Moist Deluxe Butter Recipe Golden Cake Mix
1 cup flaked coconut, divided

6 tablespoons butter or margarine, melted
¾ cup firmly packed brown sugar

1. Preheat oven to 375°F. Line two 9-inch round cake pans with aluminum foil.

2. To toast coconut, sprinkle ½ cup coconut in bottom of each pan. Bake at 375°F for about 5 minutes. Stir frequently so coconut toasts evenly.

3. Combine melted butter and sugar in medium bowl. Stir until well mixed. Spoon evenly over coconut.

4. Prepare cake following package directions. Pour batter over sugar-coconut mixture. Bake at 350°F for 30 to 35 minutes or until toothpick inserted in center comes out clean. Invert onto serving plate. Remove foil. Serve warm or at room temperature.

■ *Tip: For most recipes, unless specified, you can use either light or dark brown sugar.*

Orange No-Bake Cheesecake

Mocha Fudge Cake

12 to 16 servings

1 package Duncan Hines® Moist Deluxe
    Butter Recipe Fudge Cake Mix
1 cup hot fudge ice cream topping

1 tablespoon Folgers® Instant Coffee
4 cups frozen non-dairy whipped
    topping, thawed and divided

1. Preheat oven to 375°F. Grease and flour two 9-inch round pans.

2. Prepare, bake and cool cake following package directions.

3. For filling, combine hot fudge topping and instant coffee in medium saucepan. Heat until coffee is dissolved. Cool. Fold 2 cups whipped topping into fudge topping mixture. Refrigerate 30 minutes.

4. Place one cake layer on serving plate. Spread with 1 cup filling. Top with second cake layer. Add remaining 2 cups whipped topping to remaining filling. Frost top and sides of cake with topping mixture.

■ *Tip: Garnish with chocolate curls, chocolate-coated coffee beans or grated chocolate.*

Hummingbird Cake

12 to 16 servings

1 package Duncan Hines® Moist Deluxe
    Yellow Cake Mix
1 package (4-serving size) vanilla instant
    pudding and pie filling mix
½ cup Crisco® Oil or Puritan® Oil
1 can (8 ounces) crushed pineapple, well
    drained (reserve juice)
    Reserved pineapple juice plus water to
      equal 1 cup

4 eggs
1 teaspoon cinnamon
½ medium-size ripe banana, cut up
½ cup finely chopped pecans
¼ cup chopped maraschino cherries, well
    drained
    Confectioners sugar

1. Preheat oven to 350°F. Grease and flour 10-inch Bundt® pan.

2. Combine cake mix, pudding mix, oil, pineapple, 1 cup juice and water mixture, eggs and cinnamon in large bowl. Beat at low speed with electric mixer until moistened. Beat at medium speed for 2 minutes. Stir in banana, pecans and cherries. Pour into pan. Bake at 350°F for 50 to 60 minutes or until toothpick inserted in center comes out clean. Cool in pan 25 minutes. Invert onto serving plate. Sprinkle with confectioners sugar.

■ *Tip: Also great brushed with Cream Cheese Glaze. For glaze, follow package directions on Duncan Hines® Cream Cheese Frosting label.*

Mocha Fudge Cake

Lime Daiquiri Cake

12 to 16 servings

CAKE

1 package Duncan Hines® Moist Deluxe French Vanilla Cake Mix

3 eggs

2/3 cup water

1/3 cup lime juice

1/3 cup Crisco® Oil or Puritan® Oil

1/4 cup rum

1 teaspoon grated lime peel

3 drops green food coloring, optional

GLAZE

1/2 cup sugar

1/3 cup lime juice

1/4 cup rum

Whipped cream and twist of lime, for garnish

1. Preheat oven to 350°F. Grease and flour 10-inch Bundt® or tube pan.

2. **For cake**, combine cake mix, eggs, water, 1/3 cup lime juice, oil, 1/4 cup rum, lime peel and food coloring in large bowl. Beat at medium speed with electric mixer for 4 minutes. Pour into pan. Bake at 350°F for 45 to 50 minutes or until toothpick inserted in center comes out clean. Cool in pan 20 minutes. Invert onto serving plate. Cool 10 minutes.

3. **For glaze**, combine sugar, 1/3 cup lime juice and 1/4 cup rum. Heat and stir until sugar dissolves.

4. Poke holes in cake using skewer or long tined fork. Pour hot glaze slowly over top of cake. Cool.

5. To serve, top each slice with whipped cream and twist of lime, if desired.

■ *Tip: Extra grated lime peel or lime juice freezes well for use later.*

Mandarin Orange Cake

10 to 12 servings

CAKE

1 package Duncan Hines® Moist Deluxe Yellow Cake Mix

2 eggs

1 can (11 ounces) Mandarin orange segments, drain and reserve liquid

FILLING and FROSTING

1 package (4-serving size) vanilla instant pudding and pie filling mix

1 can (15 ounces) crushed pineapple, undrained

1 container (8 ounces) frozen non-dairy whipped topping, thawed

Additional mandarin orange segments, for garnish

1. Preheat oven to 350°F. Grease and flour two 8-inch round cake pans.

2. **For cake**, combine cake mix, eggs, drained oranges and ½ cup reserved liquid in large bowl. Beat at medium speed with electric mixer for 2 minutes. Pour into pan. Bake at 350°F for 30 minutes or until toothpick inserted in center comes out clean. Cool in pan 10 minutes. Invert onto cooling rack. Cool completely.

3. **For filling and frosting**, combine pudding mix and pineapple in medium bowl. Beat at medium speed with electric mixer for 2 minutes. Fold in whipped topping. Refrigerate 15 to 20 minutes.

4. To assemble, spread filling between cake layers and on top and sides of cake. Garnish top with additional mandarin orange segments, if desired. Refrigerate until ready to serve.

■ *Tip: To prevent cakes from picking up other flavors in the refrigerator, be sure to place cake in deep, covered cake container or cover cake with plastic wrap.*

Lime Cream Chocolate Cake   12 to 16 servings

1 package Duncan Hines® Moist Deluxe Dark Dutch Fudge Cake Mix
¼ cup sugar
2 tablespoons all-purpose flour
½ cup plus 1 tablespoon milk
1 egg, beaten
2 tablespoons lime juice
1 tablespoon butter or margarine
1 teaspoon grated lime peel
½ cup lemon yogurt
Green food coloring, optional
1 cup frozen non-dairy whipped topping, thawed

1. Preheat oven to 350°F. Grease and flour two 9-inch round cake pans.

2. Prepare, bake and cool cake following package directions.

3. Combine sugar and flour in medium saucepan. Stir in milk. Cook on medium heat, stirring constantly, until mixture thickens. Reduce heat to low. Cook 2 minutes longer. Slowly stir ½ cup mixture into beaten egg. Return mixture to saucepan. Cook until thickened. *Do not boil.* Remove from heat. Stir in lime juice, butter and peel. Cover surface with waxed paper. Cool slightly.

4. Fold yogurt into lime mixture. Add 1 or 2 drops green food coloring, if desired. Cool.

5. Place one cake layer on serving plate. Spread with thin layer of filling. Top with second layer.

6. Fold whipped topping into remaining filling. Frost top and sides of cake. Refrigerate until ready to serve.

■ *Tip: Cakes filled and frosted with whipped topping are easier to cut if you refrigerate them several hours before serving.*

Chocolate Marble Cheesecake

12 to 16 servings

CRUST

  1 package Duncan Hines® Moist Deluxe
     Devil's Food Cake Mix

½ cup Crisco® Oil or Puritan® Oil

FILLING

  3 packages (8 ounces each) cream
     cheese, softened
  ¾ cup sugar
  ½ teaspoon almond extract

3 eggs
1 square (1 ounce) unsweetened
   chocolate, melted

1. Preheat oven to 350°F. Grease 9-inch springform pan.

2. **For crust**, combine cake mix and oil in large bowl. Stir until well blended. Press mixture into bottom of pan. Bake at 350°F for 22 minutes. Remove from oven. Increase oven temperature to 450°F.

3. **For filling**, combine cream cheese, sugar and almond extract in large bowl. Beat at medium speed with electric mixer until blended. Add eggs, one at a time, beating well after each addition. Remove 1 cup filling; add melted chocolate. Spoon plain filling into warm crust. Drop spoonfuls of chocolate batter over plain batter. Run knife through batters to marble.

4. Bake at 450°F for 7 minutes. Reduce oven temperature to 250°F. Continue baking 30 minutes or until cheesecake is set. Loosen cake edge from pan. Cool before removing from pan. Refrigerate until ready to serve.

Note: Oven temperature is reduced to prevent cheesecake from cracking.

■ *Tip: To prevent chocolate from turning grainy, melt chocolate in saucepan on very low heat, or melt it in 1-cup glass measure in microwave oven at HIGH (100% power) for 1 to 1½ minutes (stir to make sure chocolate is melted).*

Chocolate Marble Cheesecake

Heavenly Chocolate Cream Pies

CRUST
- 1 package Duncan Hines® Moist Deluxe Swiss Chocolate Cake Mix
- ¾ cup butter or margarine

1st LAYER
- 1 package (8 ounces) cream cheese
- 1 cup confectioners sugar
- 1 cup frozen non-dairy whipped topping, thawed

2nd LAYER
- 2 packages (4-serving size each) chocolate instant pudding and pie filling mix
- 3 cups milk

3rd LAYER
- 2 cups frozen non-dairy whipped topping, thawed and divided

1. Preheat oven to 350°F. Grease two 9-inch pie pans.

2. **For crust**, combine cake mix and butter in large bowl. Cut butter in using pastry blender or 2 knives. Put half the crumbs in each pan. Press up sides and on bottom of each pan. Bake at 350°F for 15 minutes. Cool.

3. **For 1st layer**, combine cream cheese and confectioners sugar in small bowl. Beat at medium speed with electric mixer until smooth. Stir in 1 cup whipped topping. Spread half the mixture evenly over each crust. Refrigerate.

4. **For 2nd layer**, prepare pudding mix following package directions using 3 cups milk. Spoon half the pudding over cream cheese mixture in each pan. Refrigerate.

5. **For 3rd layer**, spread 1 cup whipped topping on each pie. Refrigerate until ready to serve.

Note: One container (8 ounces) frozen non-dairy whipped topping will be enough for recipe.

■ *Tip: For **Heavenly Lemon Cream Pies** use Duncan Hines® Moist Deluxe Lemon Supreme Cake Mix in place of Moist Deluxe Swiss Chocolate Cake Mix and lemon instant pudding and pie filling mix in place of chocolate pudding and pie filling mix.*

Heavenly Chocolate Cream Pie

Orange Coconut Fudge Cake

1 can (6 ounces) Citrus Hill® Orange
   Juice Concentrate, thawed

CAKE

1 package Duncan Hines® Moist Deluxe
   Butter Recipe Fudge Cake Mix
¾ cup Citrus Hill® Orange Juice (see step
   #2 below)

3 eggs
½ cup butter or margarine, softened
2 tablespoons orange liqueur, optional

FROSTING

1 cup evaporated milk
¾ cup sugar
3 egg yolks
¼ cup butter or margarine
2 tablespoons Citrus Hill® Frozen
   Orange Juice concentrate, thawed
   (see step #2 below)

1 teaspoon vanilla extract
2 cups chopped pecans
1 cup flaked coconut

1. Preheat oven to 375°F. Grease and flour two 9-inch round cake pans.

2. Measure 2 tablespoons orange juice concentrate. Set aside for frosting. Reconstitute remaining concentrate using ⅓ cup less water than package directions.

3. **For cake**, combine cake mix, orange juice, eggs, butter and liqueur in large bowl. Mix, bake and cool cake following package directions.

4. **For frosting**, combine evaporated milk, sugar, egg yolks and butter in medium saucepan. Cook on medium heat, stirring constantly, until mixture comes to boil and thickens. Remove from heat. Stir in reserved orange juice concentrate and vanilla extract. Add pecans and coconut. Cool. Place one cake layer on serving plate. Spread with thin layer of frosting. Top with second cake layer. Frost top and sides with remaining frosting. Refrigerate until ready to serve.

■ *Tip: Garnish cake with orange slices or twists.*

Orange Coconut Fudge Cake

Choco-Lemon Delight

1 package Duncan Hines® Moist Deluxe
   Devil's Food Cake Mix

FILLING

1 cup sugar
3 tablespoons cornstarch
⅛ teaspoon salt
1 cup water
2 egg yolks, slightly beaten
1 teaspoon grated lemon peel

2 tablespoons butter or margarine
2 tablespoons lemon juice
   Confectioners sugar
   Frozen non-dairy whipped topping,
      thawed, for garnish

1. Preheat oven to 350°F. Grease and flour two 9-inch round cake pans.

2. Prepare, bake and cool cake following package directions for original recipe.

3. **For filling**, combine sugar, cornstarch and salt in saucepan. Stir in water. Cook on medium heat, stirring constantly, until mixture comes to a full boil. Boil and stir 1 minute. Remove from heat. Gradually stir in egg yolks and lemon peel. Cook on medium heat until filling comes to boil. Reduce heat to low. Cook 1 minute. Remove from heat. Add butter. Stir until melted. Stir in lemon juice. Refrigerate 1 hour.

4. Place one cake layer on serving plate. Spread with lemon filling. Place second layer on top. Sift confectioners sugar over cake. Garnish with dollops of whipped topping around edge, if desired.

■ *Tip: One small lemon will yield about 1 teaspoon grated peel and 2 tablespoons juice.*

"Key" Lime Dessert Squares

CRUST

½ cup chopped pecans
1 package Duncan Hines® Moist Deluxe
   White Cake Mix

½ cup butter or margarine, melted

FILLING

3 egg yolks
1 can (14 ounces) sweetened condensed
   milk

⅔ cup lime juice
1 drop green food coloring, optional

TOPPING

1 container (8 ounces) frozen non-dairy
   whipped topping, thawed

1. Preheat oven to 350°F.

2. **For crust**, spread pecans in shallow baking pan. Bake 5 minutes or until lightly browned.

3. Combine pecans, cake mix and melted butter. Stir until crumbs form. Spread in bottom of ungreased 13×9×2-inch pan. Press lightly.

4. **For filling**, combine egg yolks, sweetened condensed milk, lime juice and food coloring in medium bowl. Stir until well blended. Spread over crust. Bake at 350°F for 15 minutes or until set. Cool 15 minutes. Refrigerate until chilled, about 2 hours. Cut into 2-inch squares. Serve topped with whipped topping and twist of lime, if desired.

■ *Tip: Leftover egg whites will keep refrigerated in airtight container for a few days.*

"In the Pink" Cake

12 to 16 servings

1 package Duncan Hines® Moist Deluxe
   Lemon Supreme Cake Mix
1 quart vanilla ice cream, softened
1 can (6 ounces) frozen pink lemonade
   concentrate, thawed and divided

Red food coloring
1 cup whipping cream
2 tablespoons confectioners sugar

1. Line bottom of 9-inch round cake pan with aluminum foil.

2. Combine ice cream, ⅓ cup lemonade concentrate and 5 to 6 drops food coloring. Stir until blended. Spread in foil-lined pan. Freeze until firm. Run knife around edge of pan to loosen ice cream. Remove from pan. Wrap in foil and return to freezer.

3. Preheat oven to 350°F. Grease and flour two 9-inch round cake pans.

4. Prepare, bake and cool cake following package directions. Cool completely.

5. Place one cake layer on serving plate. Place ice cream on cake. Peel off foil. Top with second cake layer. Place cake in freezer.

6. Combine whipping cream, remaining lemonade concentrate, confectioners sugar and 2 or 3 drops food coloring in medium bowl. Beat until stiff. Frost cake. Return to freezer until ready to serve.

■ *Tip: If only 12-ounce can of pink lemonade is available use ⅓ cup to blend into ice cream and ⅓ cup to mix with whipping cream. Use remaining concentrate to make lemonade using only 1½ cans of cold water.*

Double Nut Chocolate Chip Cookies

3 to 3½ dozen cookies

1 package Duncan Hines® Moist Deluxe
  Yellow Cake Mix
½ cup butter or margarine, melted
1 egg

1 cup semi-sweet chocolate chips
½ cup finely chopped pecans
1 cup sliced almonds, divided

1. Preheat oven to 375°F. Grease baking sheet.

2. Combine cake mix, melted butter and egg in large bowl. Beat at low speed with electric mixer until just blended. Stir in chocolate chips, pecans and ¼ cup sliced almonds. Shape rounded tablespoonfuls dough into balls. Place remaining ¾ cup sliced almonds in shallow bowl. Press top of cookie in almonds. Place on baking sheet, 1 inch apart.

3. Bake at 375°F for 9 to 11 minutes or until lightly browned. Cool 2 minutes on baking sheet. Remove to cooling rack.

■ *Tip: To prevent cookies from spreading too much, allow baking sheet to cool completely before baking each batch of cookies.*

Chocolate Toffee Bars

48 bars

1 package Duncan Hines® Moist Deluxe
  Yellow Cake Mix
¾ cup Butter Flavor Crisco®
1 egg

2 tablespoons milk
¾ cup semi-sweet chocolate chips
¾ cup almond brickle chips

1. Preheat oven to 350°F. Grease 13×9×2-inch pan.

2. Combine cake mix, Butter Flavor Crisco, egg and milk in large bowl. Beat at low speed with electric mixer until blended. Press into pan.

3. Bake at 350°F for 22 to 25 minutes or until lightly browned. Remove from oven. Sprinkle with chocolate chips. Return to oven for 3 more minutes. Spread melted chips evenly. Sprinkle brickle chips over chocolate. Cool. Cut into 1½×1-inch bars.

■ *Tip: You can use finely chopped nuts in place of brickle chips.*

Double Nut Chocolate Chip Cookies

Swiss Caramel Chocolate Fingers

FILLING

1 package (14 ounces) caramels	⅓ cup evaporated milk

COOKIE BASE

1 package Duncan Hines® Moist Deluxe Swiss Chocolate Cake Mix	⅓ cup evaporated milk
¾ cup butter or margarine, softened	1 package (6 ounces) semi-sweet chocolate chips

1. Preheat oven to 350°F. Grease 13×9×2-inch pan lightly.

2. **For filling**, combine caramels and milk in microwave-safe bowl. Cover with waxed paper. Microwave at MEDIUM (50% power) 2 to 3 minutes. Stir. Repeat cooking and stirring until caramels are melted and smooth (see Tip).

3. **For cookie base**, combine cake mix, butter and milk in large bowl. Beat at low speed with electric mixer until blended. Spread half of the mixture evenly in bottom of pan. Bake at 350°F for 6 minutes. Sprinkle chocolate chips evenly over baked layer. Drizzle filling over top. Use spatula or knife to spread filling to cover chips. Cool 5 minutes.

4. Drop remaining cookie base mixture by half teaspoonfuls evenly over filling. Use back of spoon to gently spread cookie base to cover filling. Return to oven. Bake at 350°F for 17 to 22 minutes or until top looks dry. Mixture will not appear firm. Cool. Refrigerate for 30 minutes. Cut into bars.

■ *Tip: Caramels and evaporated milk can be combined in heavy saucepan. Cook and stir on low heat until caramels are melted and smooth.*

Spicy Sour Cream Cookies

4½ dozen cookies

1 package Duncan Hines® Moist Deluxe Spice Cake Mix	1 cup chopped pecans or walnuts
1 cup dairy sour cream	¼ cup butter or margarine, softened
	1 egg

1. Preheat oven to 350°F. Grease baking sheets.

2. Combine cake mix, sour cream, pecans, butter and egg in large bowl. Beat at low speed with electric mixer until blended.

3. Drop by rounded teaspoonfuls onto baking sheet. Bake at 350°F for 9 to 11 minutes or until lightly browned. Cool 2 minutes on baking sheet. Remove to cooling rack.

■ *Tip: Sprinkle cookies with confectioners sugar.*

Swiss Caramel Chocolate Fingers

Strawberries and Cream Cheesecake Tarts

24 mini cheesecakes

CRUST

1 package Duncan Hines® Moist Deluxe Strawberry Supreme Cake Mix

¼ cup butter or margarine, melted

FILLING

2 packages (8 ounces each) cream cheese, softened

3 eggs

¾ cup sugar

1 teaspoon vanilla extract

TOPPING

1½ cups dairy sour cream

¼ cup sugar

12 fresh strawberries

1. Preheat oven to 350°F. Place 2½-inch foil liners in 24 muffin cups.

2. **For crust**, combine cake mix and melted butter in large bowl. Beat at low speed with electric mixer for 1 minute. Divide mixture evenly in muffin cups. Level but do not press.

3. **For filling**, combine cream cheese, eggs, ¾ cup sugar and vanilla extract in medium bowl. Beat at medium speed with electric mixer until smooth. Spoon evenly into muffin cups.

4. Bake at 350°F for 20 minutes or until mixture is set.

5. **For topping**, combine sour cream and ¼ cup sugar in small bowl. Spoon evenly over cheesecakes. Return to oven for 5 minutes. Cool.

6. Garnish each cheesecake with strawberry half. Refrigerate until ready to serve.

■ *Tip: If you use dark colored muffin pans, reduce the oven temperature to 325°F to prevent over-baking the tarts.*

Oatmeal Applesauce Squares

12 bars

1 package Duncan Hines® Moist Deluxe Spice Cake Mix	2 cups applesauce
2 eggs	1 cup quick-cooking oats (not instant or old-fashioned)
½ cup butter or margarine, softened	½ cup firmly packed brown sugar

1. Preheat oven to 350°F. Grease 13×9×2-inch pan.

2. Combine cake mix, eggs and butter in large bowl. Beat at low speed with electric mixer until blended. Spread in pan.

3. Bake at 350°F for 15 minutes. Pour applesauce over baked layer.

4. Combine oats and brown sugar in small bowl. Mix until crumbly. Sprinkle over applesauce. Return to oven. Bake at 350°F for 10 minutes or until lightly browned. Cool. Cut into 3-inch squares.

■ *Tip: You can use flavored applesauce in place of regular applesauce.*

Lemon Bars

32 bars

1 package Duncan Hines® Moist Deluxe Lemon Supreme Cake Mix	¼ cup lemon juice
3 eggs, divided	2 teaspoons grated lemon peel
⅓ cup Butter Flavor Crisco®	½ teaspoon baking powder
½ cup sugar	¼ teaspoon salt
	Confectioners sugar

1. Preheat oven to 350°F.

2. Combine cake mix, 1 egg and Butter Flavor Crisco in large bowl. Beat at low speed with electric mixer until crumbs form. Reserve 1 cup. Pat remaining mixture lightly into ungreased 13×9×2-inch pan.

3. Bake at 350°F for 15 minutes or until lightly browned.

4. Combine remaining 2 eggs, sugar, lemon juice, lemon peel, baking powder and salt in medium bowl. Beat at medium speed with electric mixer until light and foamy. Pour over hot crust. Sprinkle with reserved crumb mixture.

5. Bake at 350°F for 15 minutes or until lightly browned. Sprinkle with confectioners sugar. Cool. Cut into bars.

■ *Tip: For **Lime Bars**, you can use lime juice and lime peel in place of lemon juice and lemon peel.*

Oatmeal Applesauce Squares

Pinwheel Cookies

3½ dozen cookies

½ cup Butter Flavor Crisco®
⅓ cup plus 1 tablespoon butter, softened
   and divided
2 egg yolks

½ teaspoon vanilla extract
1 package Duncan Hines® Moist Deluxe
   Fudge Marble Cake Mix

1. Combine Butter Flavor Crisco, ⅓ cup butter, egg yolks and vanilla extract in large bowl. Beat at low speed with electric mixer until blended. Set aside cocoa packet. Gradually add cake mix. Blend well.

2. Divide dough. Add cocoa packet and remaining 1 tablespoon butter to half the dough. Knead until well blended and chocolate colored.

3. Roll out yellow dough between two pieces of waxed paper into 18×12×⅛-inch rectangle. Repeat for chocolate dough. Remove top pieces of waxed paper from chocolate dough and yellow dough. Lay yellow dough directly on top of chocolate. Remove remaining layers of waxed paper. Roll up jelly-roll fashion, beginning at wide side. Refrigerate 2 hours.

4. Preheat oven to 350°F. Grease baking sheets.

5. Cut dough into ⅛-inch slices. Bake at 350°F for 9 to 11 minutes or until lightly browned. Cool 5 minutes on baking sheets. Remove to cooling rack.

■ *Tip: You can use Duncan Hines® Moist Deluxe White Cake Mix in place of Fudge Marble Cake Mix. Divide dough as above; color one portion of dough with red or green food coloring.*

Peanut Butter Chocolate Chip Cookies

4 dozen cookies

1 package Duncan Hines® Moist Deluxe
   Yellow Cake Mix
½ cup Jif® Creamy Peanut Butter

½ cup butter or margarine, softened
2 eggs
1 cup milk chocolate chips

1. Preheat oven to 350°F. Grease baking sheets.

2. Combine cake mix, peanut butter, butter and eggs in large bowl. Beat at low speed with electric mixer until blended. Stir in chocolate chips.

3. Drop by rounded teaspoonfuls onto baking sheet. Bake at 350°F for 9 to 11 minutes or until lightly browned. Cool 2 minutes on baking sheet. Remove to cooling rack.

■ *Tip: You can use Jif® Extra Crunchy Peanut Butter in place of regular peanut butter.*

Pinwheel Cookies

Lemon Cookies

1 package Duncan Hines® Moist Deluxe
  Lemon Supreme Cake Mix
2 eggs
⅓ cup Crisco® Oil or Puritan® Oil

1 tablespoon lemon juice
¾ cup chopped nuts or flaked coconut
  Confectioners sugar

1. Preheat oven to 375°F. Grease baking sheets.

2. Combine cake mix, eggs, oil and lemon juice in large bowl. Beat at low speed with electric mixer until well blended. Add nuts. Shape into 1-inch balls. Place on baking sheet, 1 inch apart. Bake at 375°F for 6 or 7 minutes or until lightly browned. Cool 1 minute on baking sheet. Remove to cooling rack. Dust with confectioners sugar.

■ *Tip: You can frost cookies with 1 cup confectioners sugar mixed with 1 tablespoon lemon juice in place of dusting cookies with confectioners sugar.*

Raspberry Meringue Bars

BASE

1 package Duncan Hines® Moist Deluxe
  Yellow Cake Mix

½ cup butter or margarine, melted
2 egg yolks

TOPPING

2 egg whites
½ cup sugar
1 cup chopped walnuts

1 cup raspberry preserves
½ cup flaked coconut

1. Preheat oven to 350°F.

2. **For base**, combine cake mix, melted butter and egg yolks in large bowl. Beat at low speed with electric mixer for 1 minute. Spread in ungreased 13×9×2-inch pan.

3. Bake at 350°F for 15 minutes or until lightly browned.

4. **For topping**, beat egg whites in medium bowl at high speed with electric mixer until foamy and double in volume. Beat in sugar. Continue beating until meringue forms firm peaks. Fold in walnuts.

5. Spread raspberry preserves over crust. Sprinkle with coconut. Spread meringue over top.

6. Bake at 350°F for 25 minutes. Cool in pan. Cut into bars.

■ *Tip: You can use other flavor preserves in place of raspberry.*

Lemon Cookies

Quick and Easy Nutty Cheese Bars

BASE

1 package Duncan Hines® Moist Deluxe Butter Recipe Golden Cake Mix	¾ cup chopped pecans or walnuts ¾ cup butter or margarine, melted

TOPPING

2 packages (8 ounces each) cream cheese, softened	1 cup firmly packed brown sugar ¾ cup chopped pecans or walnuts

1. Preheat oven to 350°F. Grease and flour 13×9×2-inch pan.

2. **For base**, combine cake mix, ¾ cup pecans and melted butter in large bowl. Stir until well blended. Press mixture into bottom of pan.

3. **For topping**, combine cream cheese and brown sugar in medium bowl. Stir with spoon until well mixed. Spread evenly over base. Sprinkle with ¾ cup pecans.

4. Bake at 350°F for 25 to 30 minutes or until edges are browned and cheese topping is set. Cool completely. Cut into bars. Refrigerate leftovers.

■ *Tip: For successful baking, using the correct measuring cup is important. A lipped measuring cup is for measuring liquids and a flush rimmed cup is for measuring dry ingredients.*

Fudge Marble Bars

1 package Duncan Hines® Moist Deluxe Fudge Marble Cake Mix ¼ cup plus 1 tablespoon water, divided 2 eggs	¼ cup butter or margarine, softened 1 cup semi-sweet chocolate chips ½ cup chopped pecans

1. Preheat oven to 350°F. Grease 13×9×2-inch pan.

2. Set aside cocoa packet. Combine cake mix, ¼ cup water, eggs and butter in large bowl. Beat at low speed with electric mixer until just blended.

3. Measure ½ cup batter into small bowl. Add cocoa packet, chocolate chips and remaining 1 tablespoon water. Stir until blended.

4. Add pecans to yellow batter. Spread in pan. Spoon chocolate batter on top. Run knife through batters to marble.

5. Bake at 350°F for 22 to 27 minutes or until toothpick inserted in center comes out clean. Cool. Cut into bars.

■ *Tip: For **Fudge Marble Mint Bars**, use mint chocolate chips in place of semi-sweet chocolate chips.*

Quick and Easy Nutty Cheese Bars

Chocolate Peanut Butter Cookies

3½ dozen cookies

1 package Duncan Hines® Moist Deluxe
   Devil's Food Cake Mix
¾ cup Jif® Extra Crunchy Peanut Butter

2 eggs
2 tablespoons milk
1 cup candy-coated peanut butter pieces

1. Preheat oven to 350°F. Grease baking sheets.

2. Combine cake mix, peanut butter, eggs and milk in large bowl. Beat at low speed with electric mixer until blended. Stir in peanut butter pieces.

3. Drop by slightly rounded tablespoonfuls onto baking sheet. Bake at 350°F for 7 to 9 minutes or until lightly browned. Cool 2 minutes on baking sheet. Remove to cooling rack.

■ *Tip: You can use 1 cup peanut butter flavored chips in place of peanut butter pieces.*

Swiss Chocolate Crispies

4 dozen cookies

1 package Duncan Hines® Moist Deluxe
   Swiss Chocolate Cake Mix
½ cup Butter Flavor Crisco®
½ cup butter or margarine, softened

2 eggs
2 tablespoons water
3 cups crisp rice cereal, divided

1. Combine cake mix, Butter Flavor Crisco, butter, eggs and water in large bowl. Beat at low speed with electric mixer for 2 minutes. Fold in 1 cup cereal. Refrigerate 1 hour.

2. Crush remaining 2 cups cereal into coarse crumbs.

3. Preheat oven to 350°F. Grease baking sheets.

4. Shape dough into 1-inch balls. Roll in crushed cereal. Place on baking sheets about 1 inch apart.

5. Bake at 350°F for 11 to 13 minutes or until lightly browned. Cool 1 minute on baking sheets. Remove to cooling rack.

■ *Tip: For evenly baked cookies, place baking sheet in center of oven, not touching sides.*

Chocolate Peanut Butter Cookies

Jelly Roll Diploma

8 to 10 servings

1 package Duncan Hines® Angel Food
   Cake Mix
1 cup water
¾ cup Crisco® Oil or Puritan® Oil
¼ cup all-purpose flour
3 eggs

½ teaspoon vanilla extract
2 tablespoons grated lemon peel
   Confectioners sugar
⅔ cup any red jam or preserves
   Ribbon for bow

1. Preheat oven to 350°F. Line a 15½×10½×1-inch jelly-roll pan with waxed paper and grease the waxed paper. Place 2½-inch paper or foil liners in 24 muffin cups.*

2. Combine water and egg white packet (blue) in large bowl. Beat at low speed with electric mixer for 1 minute. Beat at high speed until very stiff peaks form. Combine flour packet (red), oil, flour, eggs, vanilla extract and lemon peel in medium bowl. Beat at low speed until blended. Beat at medium speed for 3 minutes. Fold beaten egg whites into yellow batter. Pour enough batter into jelly-roll pan to fill to within one-fourth inch of top. Spread evenly.

3. Bake at 350°F about 30 minutes, or until toothpick inserted in center comes out clean. Immediately invert cake onto dish towel covered with confectioners sugar. Peel off paper and trim edges of cake. Roll up with towel jelly-roll fashion. Cool. Unroll cake and spread with jam. Reroll. Sprinkle top with confectioners sugar. Tie a ribbon around diploma.

*For cupcakes, while jelly roll cake is baking, spoon remaining batter into muffin cups, filling each about two-thirds full. Bake at 350°F for 15 to 20 minutes. Cool. Frost as desired. Makes 24 cupcakes.

■ *Tip: For Graduation prediction cupcakes write predictions such as "Your job interview will be a winner" on small piece of white paper. Roll up. Tuck paper in small cut in bottom of each cake. Frost as desired.*

Jelly Roll Diploma

Blueberry Coffee Cake

12 servings

CRUST

1 package Duncan Hines® Moist Deluxe
    Yellow Cake Mix
½ cup butter or margarine, softened

2 eggs, beaten
⅓ cup milk
1 teaspoon vanilla extract

FILLING

3 cups fresh blueberries
⅔ cup sugar

2 tablespoons all-purpose flour
⅛ teaspoon cinnamon

TOPPING

2 cups fresh blueberries
1 cup orange marmalade

1 teaspoon lemon juice

1. Preheat oven to 375°F. Grease and flour 13×9×2-inch pan.

2. **For crust**, combine cake mix and butter in large bowl. Cut butter into cake mix using pastry blender or two knives until coarse crumbs form. Add eggs, milk and vanilla extract. Stir with fork until smooth. Spread batter evenly in bottom and 1 inch up sides of pan.

3. **For filling**, sprinkle 3 cups blueberries over crust. Combine sugar, flour and cinnamon. Sprinkle over blueberries. Bake at 375°F for 40 to 50 minutes or until golden brown.

4. **For topping**, sprinkle 2 cups blueberries over warm cake. Heat marmalade and lemon juice in small saucepan. Spoon over blueberries. Cool slightly. Cut into 3-inch squares.

■ *Tip: Serve warm or at room temperature. Top with whipped cream or ice cream, if desired.*

Father's Day Tie

12 to 16 servings

1 package Duncan Hines® Moist Deluxe
    Cake Mix (any flavor)
1 container (16 ounces) Duncan Hines®
    Vanilla Layer Cake Frosting

Food coloring
Colored sugar crystals

1. Preheat oven to 350°F. Grease and flour 13×9×2-inch pan.

2. Prepare, bake and cool cake following package directions. Invert cake onto large tray.

3. Frost sides and top of cake with vanilla frosting. Tint remaining frosting with food coloring. Outline shirt collar and tie on cake with colored frosting using decorator's tube (see Tip). Create your own design on tie with colored sugars and frosting. Personalize with frosting monogram or name, if desired.

■ *Tip: If decorator's tube is not available, place about ⅓ cup tinted frosting in small airtight plastic bag. Seal top and cut off a tiny bottom corner to use as tip. Refill as needed.*

Blueberry Coffee Cake

Harvey Wallbanger's Cake

12 to 16 servings

1 package Duncan Hines® Moist Deluxe
  Orange Supreme Cake Mix
3 eggs
¾ cup Citrus Hill® Orange Juice

⅓ cup Crisco® Oil or Puritan® Oil
⅓ cup Galliano®
¼ cup vodka
Confectioners sugar

1. Preheat oven to 350°F. Grease and flour 10-inch Bundt® pan.

2. Combine cake mix, eggs, orange juice, oil, Galliano and vodka in large bowl. Beat at medium speed with electric mixer for 4 minutes. Pour into pan. Bake at 350°F for 45 to 50 minutes, or until toothpick inserted in center comes out clean. Cool in pan 25 minutes. Invert onto serving plate. Cool completely. Dust with confectioners sugar.

■ *Tip: For a non-alcoholic cake, use ½ cup plus 1 tablespoon water in place of Galliano and vodka.*

Baked Alaska

10 to 12 servings

½ gallon ice cream, softened

1 package Duncan Hines® Moist Deluxe
  White Cake Mix

MERINGUE

4 egg whites, at room temperature
½ teaspoon cream of tartar

¾ cup sugar
½ teaspoon vanilla extract

1. Line 2-quart round bowl with plastic wrap. Press softened ice cream into bowl. Freeze until firm.

2. Preheat oven to 350°F. Grease and flour two 8-inch round cake pans.

3. Prepare, bake and cool cake following package directions. Place one layer on heatproof platter. (Freeze other layer in airtight plastic bag for a quick dessert at a later time.)

4. **For meringue**, beat egg whites in medium bowl at high speed with electric mixer until foamy. Add cream of tartar. Gradually beat in sugar. Add vanilla extract. Beat 5 minutes or until thick and glossy.

5. To assemble, unmold ice cream on top of cake layer. Remove plastic wrap. Spread meringue over ice cream and cake. Cover completely. Return to freezer for 15 minutes.

6. Reheat oven to 450°F. Bake Alaska 4 or 5 minutes or until lightly browned. Serve immediately.

■ *Tip: Baked Alaska can be assembled earlier in the day and frozen. Bake meringue at serving time; or bake ahead and freeze until ready to serve.*

White Chocolate Mousse with Raspberry Sauce

12 servings

1 package Duncan Hines® Moist Deluxe
  Devil's Food Cake Mix

MOUSSE

1 envelope unflavored gelatin

2¼ cups whipping cream, divided

6 ounces white chocolate bars

½ teaspoon almond extract

2 tablespoons sugar

SAUCE

2 cups fresh or frozen, thawed
  raspberries

3 tablespoons sugar

1. Preheat oven to 350°F. Grease and flour 13×9×2-inch pan.

2. Prepare, bake and cool cake following package directions.

3. **For mousse**, sprinkle gelatin over 1¼ cups whipping cream in medium saucepan. Let stand 5 minutes. Add white chocolate. Cook on low heat, stirring constantly, until chocolate is melted and mixture is smooth. Transfer to large bowl. Refrigerate 10 minutes, stirring occasionally. Beat remaining 1 cup whipping cream and almond extract in small bowl. Gradually add 2 tablespoons sugar. Beat until stiff. Fold into chocolate mixture. Spread over cooled cake. Refrigerate for 2 hours.

4. Reserve 1 cup whole raspberries for garnish. **For sauce**, combine remaining raspberries and 3 tablespoons sugar in small saucepan. Bring to boil. Simmer until berries are soft. Push mixture through sieve into small bowl. Set aside to cool.

5. Cut cake into 3-inch squares. Place on individual plates. Drizzle raspberry sauce over squares. Garnish with whole raspberries.

■ *Tip: You can also serve the dessert by spooning the raspberry sauce onto dessert plates. Then place each cake square on top of the sauce and decorate with reserved raspberries.*

Easter Basket Cupcakes

1 package Duncan Hines® Moist Deluxe
   Yellow Cake Mix
3 tablespoons plus 1½ teaspoons water
6 drops green food coloring
1½ cups shredded coconut

1 container (16 ounces) Duncan Hines®
   Vanilla Layer Cake Frosting
½ pound assorted colors jelly beans
24 assorted colors pipe cleaners

1. Preheat oven to 350°F. Place 2½-inch paper liners in 24 muffin cups.

2. Prepare, bake and cool cupcakes following package directions.

3. Combine water and green food coloring in large container with tight fitting lid. Add coconut. Shake until coconut is evenly tinted green.

4. Frost cupcakes with vanilla frosting. Sprinkle coconut over frosting. Press 3 jelly beans into coconut on each cupcake. Bend pipe cleaners to form handles. Push into cupcakes.

■ *Tip: You can make fruit baskets by placing fruit slices on top of frosting in place of coconut and jelly beans.*

Fruit Parfaits

1 package Duncan Hines® Moist Deluxe
   Yellow Cake Mix
2 cups fresh peaches, peeled and diced
1 cup miniature marshmallows
¼ cup flaked coconut

1½ cups whipping cream
2 tablespoons confectioners sugar
½ teaspoon almond extract
6 peach slices

1. Preheat oven to 350°F. Grease and flour two 9-inch round cake pans.

2. Prepare, bake and cool cake following package directions.

3. Cut one cake layer into 1-inch cubes. Place in large bowl. (Freeze other cake in large airtight plastic bag to use later.) Add diced peaches, marshmallows and coconut to cake. Toss to mix.

4. Combine whipping cream, confectioners sugar and almond extract in large bowl. Beat at high speed with electric mixer until stiff. Set aside enough whipped cream for garnish. Fold remaining whipped cream into cake mixture. Spoon into 6 parfait dishes. Top each with reserved whipped cream and peach slice. Refrigerate until ready to serve.

■ *Tip: For a quick dessert, defrost frozen cake and cut cake in half vertically. Frost one half. Stack other half on top. Frost uncut sides and top for half a cake, which will serve 6 to 8.*

Easter Basket Cupcakes

Rainbow Sorbet Torte

10 to 12 servings

4 pints assorted flavors sorbet
1 package Duncan Hines® Moist Deluxe
   White Cake Mix

Assorted fruit, for garnish

1. Line bottom of 8-inch round cake pan with aluminum foil. Soften one pint of sorbet. Spread evenly in pan. Return to freezer until firm. Run knife around edge of pan to loosen sorbet. Remove from pan. Wrap in foil and return to freezer. Repeat for other flavors.

2. Preheat oven to 350°F. Grease and flour two 8-inch round cake pans.

3. Prepare, bake and cool cake following package directions for No Cholesterol recipe.

4. To assemble torte, cut both cake layers in half horizontally. Place one cake layer on serving plate. Top with one layer sorbet. Peel off foil. Repeat for all cake and sorbet layers. Wrap aluminum foil around plate and cake. Return to freezer until ready to serve. To serve, garnish top with fruit.

■ *Tip: This is a good make-ahead dessert. Whole torte can be served or you may use only a few slices at a time.*

Spicy Oatmeal Raisin Cookies

4 dozen cookies

1 package Duncan Hines® Moist Deluxe
   Spice Cake Mix
4 egg whites
1 cup quick-cooking oats (not instant or
   old-fashioned)

½ cup Crisco® Oil or Puritan® Oil
½ cup raisins

1. Preheat oven to 350°F. Grease baking sheets.

2. Combine cake mix, egg whites, oats and oil in large bowl. Beat at low speed with electric mixer until blended. Stir in raisins. Drop by rounded teaspoons onto baking sheets.

3. Bake at 350°F for 7 to 9 minutes or until lightly browned. Cool 1 minute on baking sheets. Remove to cooling rack.

■ *Tip: You may use other Duncan Hines® cake mix flavors in place of Spice Cake Mix.*

Rainbow Sorbet Torte

Strawberry Basket

1 package Duncan Hines® Moist Deluxe
    White Cake Mix

GLAZE

3 cups medium-size strawberries, divided

⅓ cup water

¼ cup sugar

1 tablespoon cornstarch

Red food coloring

FROSTING

1 container (16 ounces) Duncan Hines®
    Vanilla Layer Cake Frosting

1 tablespoon plus 2 teaspoons cocoa

1. Preheat oven to 350°F. Grease and flour two 8-inch square pans.

2. Prepare, bake and cool cake following package directions for No Cholesterol recipe.

3. **For glaze**, wash berries. Remove stems and leaves. Simmer ½ cup berries with water for 2 minutes in small saucepan. Push mixture through sieve into small bowl. Return to saucepan. Combine sugar and cornstarch in small cup. Add to berry juice. Cook until glaze is thickened and clear. Stir in 3 drops food coloring. Set aside.

4. **For frosting**, mix vanilla frosting and cocoa until smooth in small bowl.

5. To assemble, place one layer on serving plate. Frost with ⅓ cup cocoa frosting. Top with second layer. Cut into top of cake 1 inch in from all four edges; cut down 1 inch deep. Lift out cut section with pancake turner. (One inch rim will be left on top layer.) Frost outside and top rim of cake with cocoa frosting. Spoon 2 tablespoons glaze in cut out area. Spread evenly. Fill with remaining strawberries, pointed ends up. Brush berries with remaining glaze. Make basket pattern in frosting using four-tine fork.

■ *Tip: For a delicious snack, spread leftover frosting between graham crackers.*

Mexican Chocolate Cake

1 package Duncan Hines® Moist Deluxe
    Dark Dutch Fudge Cake Mix

1 teaspoon cinnamon

1 container (16 ounces) Duncan Hines®
    Dark Dutch Fudge Layer Cake
    Frosting

1. Preheat oven to 350°F. Grease and flour two 9-inch round cake pans.

2. Prepare, bake and cool cake following package directions for No Cholesterol recipe.

3. Stir cinnamon into dark dutch fudge frosting; frost tops and sides of cake.

■ *Tip: Always use a cooling rack to cool cake layers. If you place warm cake layers on a plate to cool, the cake will become soggy and stick to the plate.*

Strawberry Basket

Amaretto Apricot Cake

12 to 16 servings

1 package Duncan Hines® Moist Deluxe
White Cake Mix

FILLING

1 jar (12 ounces) apricot preserves

2 tablespoons Amaretto liqueur

TOPPING

3 cups frozen non-dairy whipped
topping, thawed
Apricot halves

Toasted slivered almonds
(see Tip, page 79)

1. Preheat oven to 350°F. Grease and flour two 8-inch round cake pans.

2. Prepare, bake and cool cake following package directions for No Cholesterol recipe. Refrigerate layers 1 hour. Cut each layer in half horizontally (see Tip).

3. **For filling**, combine apricot preserves and Amaretto in small bowl; stir well.

4. To assemble, place one cake layer on serving plate. Spread with one-third of apricot mixture. Repeat with 2 more layers. Place remaining layer on top.

5. **For topping**, frost cake with whipped topping. Garnish with apricot halves and almond slivers.

■ *Tip: To cut evenly, measure cake with ruler. Divide into 2 equal layers. Mark with toothpicks. Cut through layers using toothpicks as guide.*

Chocolate Cake with Strawberry Whip and Chocolate-Dipped Strawberries

12 to 16 servings

1 package Duncan Hines® Moist Deluxe
Devil's Food Cake Mix

CHOCOLATE-DIPPED STRAWBERRIES

1 pint fresh strawberries with stems
1 cup semi-sweet chocolate chips

1 tablespoon Crisco® Shortening

STRAWBERRY WHIP

1 package (10 ounces) sliced frozen
strawberries, thawed

1 container (8 ounces) frozen non-dairy
whipped topping, thawed

1. Preheat oven to 350°F. Grease and flour 10-inch tube pan.

2. Prepare, bake and cool cake following package directions for No Cholesterol recipe.

3. **For chocolate-dipped strawberries**, rinse and thoroughly dry strawberries (see Tip). Place a piece of waxed paper under a cooling rack.

4. Melt chocolate chips and Crisco on very low heat in small saucepan. Or melt chips in microwave oven; place in 4-cup glass measure and microwave at MEDIUM (50% power) for 1 to 1½ minutes. Stir to combine. Hold strawberries by stems. Dip ends into melted chocolate. Allow excess to drip off. Turn upside down (stem-side down) on cooling rack.

5. **For strawberry whip**, using spatula, fold frozen strawberries into whipped topping in large bowl.

6. To serve, place slice of cake on serving plate. Top with strawberry whip. Garnish with whole or halved chocolate-dipped strawberries.

■ *Tip: When melting chocolate be sure to avoid getting any water into the chocolate mixture. (Strawberries should be* completely *dry.) Water will cause the chocolate mixture to turn grainy and to stiffen. If chocolate becomes too thick for easy dipping, thin it by reheating and adding a small amount of Crisco.*

Angel Food Cake with Chocolate Sauce   12 to 16 servings

1 package Duncan Hines® Angel Food
   Cake Mix

SAUCE
   1 container (16 ounces) Duncan Hines®   1 cup chopped pecans or walnuts
      Milk Chocolate Layer Cake Frosting   ½ cup water

1. Preheat oven to 375°F.

2. Prepare, bake and cool cake following package directions.

3. **For sauce**, reheat oven to 350°F. Spread pecans in shallow pan. Bake at 350°F for about 5 minutes. (Watch closely as they can burn quickly.) Stir occasionally.

4. Combine milk chocolate frosting, pecans and water in small saucepan. Warm on low heat. Serve over slices of cake.

■ *Tip: The best way to cut angel food cakes is to use a long serrated knife and cut with a light sawing motion.*

Raspberry Swirl Cake

12 to 16 servings

1 package Duncan Hines® Moist Deluxe
French Vanilla Cake Mix

RASPBERRY SAUCE

1 package (12 ounces) frozen
raspberries, thawed
2 tablespoons seedless raspberry jam
1 tablespoon cornstarch

1 tablespoon water
1 container (16 ounces) Duncan Hines®
Cream Cheese Layer Cake Frosting

1. Preheat oven to 350°F. Grease and flour two 9-inch round cake pans.

2. Prepare, bake and cool cake following package directions for No Cholesterol recipe.

3. **For raspberry sauce**, place sieve over small saucepan. Push raspberries through sieve with spoon. Discard seeds. Add jam. Dissolve cornstarch in water in small cup. Add to saucepan. Cook on medium heat, stirring constantly, until sauce comes to boil and thickens. Cool.

4. To assemble, place one cake layer (bottom-side up) on plate. Spread with raspberry sauce, reserving enough to drizzle on top. Place second layer on top. Frost sides and top of cake with cream cheese frosting. Drizzle with remaining sauce. Run knife through frosting and sauce to swirl.

■ *Tip: You may use strawberries and strawberry jam in place of the raspberries and raspberry jam.*

Refrigerated Peach Sheet Cake

12 servings

1 package Duncan Hines® Moist Deluxe
White Cake Mix
1 package (4-serving size) peach flavored
gelatin

1 cup boiling water
1 container (8 ounces) frozen non-dairy
whipped topping, thawed
1 medium peach, sliced

1. Preheat oven to 350°F. Grease and flour 13×9×2-inch pan.

2. Prepare and bake cake following package directions for No Cholesterol recipe. Cool 5 minutes.

3. Dissolve gelatin in boiling water in small bowl. Cool until slightly thickened.

4. Poke holes in top of cake with toothpick or long-tined fork. Gradually pour gelatin mixture over cake. Refrigerate for 2 hours.

5. To serve, frost cake with whipped topping. Garnish with peach slices. Cut into 3-inch squares.

■ *Tip: You can use other flavors of gelatin and fresh fruit, such as apricot, raspberry or strawberry.*

Raspberry Swirl Cake

Fantasy Angel Food Cake

16 servings

1 package Duncan Hines® Angel Food
   Cake Mix
Red and green food coloring

1 container (16 ounces) Duncan Hines®
   Cream Cheese Layer Cake Frosting

1. Preheat oven to 375°F.

2. Prepare cake following package directions. Divide batter into thirds and place in 3 different bowls. Add a few drops red food coloring to one. Add a few drops green food coloring to another. Stir each until well blended. Leave the third one plain. Spoon pink batter into ungreased 10-inch tube pan. Cover with white batter and top with green batter. Bake and cool following package directions.

3. Follow directions on frosting label for Cream Cheese Glaze. Glaze top and sides of cake. Divide remaining glaze in half and place in 2 different bowls. Add a few drops red food coloring to one. Add a few drops green food coloring to the other. Stir each until well blended. Using a teaspoon, drizzle green glaze around edge of cake so it will run down sides. Repeat with pink glaze.

■ *Tip: For marble cake, run knife through batters.*

Lemon-Orange Angel Food Cake with Sauce

12 to 16 servings

CAKE

1 package Duncan Hines® Angel Food
   Cake Mix

2 tablespoons grated lemon peel
1 tablespoon grated orange peel

SAUCE

1 container (16 ounces) Duncan Hines®
   Vanilla Layer Cake Frosting
¼ cup Citrus Hill® Frozen Orange Juice
   concentrate

2 tablespoons lemon juice
1 teaspoon grated orange peel

1. Preheat oven to 375°F.

2. **For cake**, prepare cake following package directions. Add lemon peel and 1 tablespoon orange peel to batter. Bake and cool as directed.

3. **For sauce**, combine vanilla frosting, orange juice concentrate, lemon juice and 1 teaspoon orange peel in small bowl. Stir until smooth. Serve over cake slices.

■ *Tip: To make orange juice from remaining concentrate, add 3 times the amount of water to concentrate.*

Fantasy Angel Food Cake

Piña Colada Cake

16 servings

1 package Duncan Hines® Moist Deluxe
Pineapple Supreme Cake Mix

FILLING

2 cups milk

1 package (8 ounces) cream cheese,
softened

1 package (4-serving size) vanilla instant
pudding and pie filling mix

¾ teaspoon rum flavoring or extract

1 can (8½ ounces) crushed pineapple,
well drained

TOPPING

2 cups frozen non-dairy whipped
topping, thawed

½ cup flaked coconut, for garnish

½ cup pineapple tidbits, for garnish

½ cup maraschino cherries, for garnish

1. Preheat oven to 350°F. Grease and flour 10-inch tube pan.

2. Prepare, bake and cool cake following package directions for original recipe.

3. Cut cooled cake into three equal layers (see Tip).

4. **For filling**, combine milk, cream cheese, pudding mix and flavoring in small bowl. Beat at medium speed with electric mixer for 2 minutes.

5. To assemble, place one cake layer on serving plate. Spread with half the pudding mixture. Top with half the crushed pineapple. Repeat with second cake layer and remaining filling. Place third cake layer on top.

6. **For topping**, spread whipped topping on sides and top of cake. Refrigerate until ready to serve. Garnish with coconut, pineapple tidbits and cherries, if desired.

■ *Tip: To cut cake evenly, measure cake with ruler. Divide into 3 equal layers. Mark with toothpicks. Cut through layers using toothpicks as guide.*

Piña Colada Cake

Orange Sunshine Cake

12 to 16 servings

1 package Duncan Hines® Moist Deluxe
  Orange Supreme Cake Mix

FILLING

1¼ cups sugar
 5 tablespoons cornstarch
 ⅔ cup water

½ cup Citrus Hill® Orange Juice
1 teaspoon grated orange peel
  Red and yellow food coloring

FROSTING

1 cup whipping cream

2 tablespoons confectioners sugar

1. Preheat oven to 350°F. Grease and flour two 9-inch round cake pans.

2. Prepare, bake and cool cake following package directions.

3. **For filling,** combine sugar and cornstarch in small saucepan. Stir in water, orange juice and peel. Cook on medium heat, stirring constantly, until mixture thickens and turns translucent. Remove from heat. Stir in a few drops of each food coloring to achieve orange color. Refrigerate 2 hours.

4. Place one cake layer on serving plate. Spread with half of orange filling. Top with second layer. Spread remaining filling on top to within 1 inch of edge.

5. **For frosting,** beat whipping cream until soft peaks form in large bowl. Gradually add confectioners sugar. Beat until stiff peaks form. Frost sides and remaining edge of top with whipped cream, leaving filling in center uncovered. Refrigerate until ready to serve.

■ *Tip: Garnish with fresh orange cut into thin slices or into twists.*

Peach Melba Upside Down Cake

12 servings

1 package Duncan Hines® Moist Deluxe
  Lemon Supreme Cake Mix
1 cup butter or margarine, softened and
  divided
1½ cups firmly packed brown sugar

1 can (29 ounces) sliced peaches in heavy
  syrup, drained, with juice reserved
1 cup fresh or frozen raspberries, thawed
3 eggs

1. Preheat oven to 375°F. Line bottom of 13×9×2-inch baking pan with aluminum foil.

2. Melt ½ cup butter in small saucepan. Add brown sugar. Stir until dissolved. Spread in bottom of pan. Arrange 1 peach slice and 3 raspberries as if for 12 individual servings.

3. Combine cake mix, 1 cup peach juice, eggs and remaining ½ cup butter in large bowl. Stir until thoroughly combined. Pour cake batter over fruit. Bake at 375°F for 35 to 40 minutes or until lightly browned. Remove from oven. Invert onto serving tray. Remove pan. Remove foil. Cool. Use fruit as guide to cut into individual servings.

■ *Tip: You can use fresh or frozen blueberries in place of raspberries.*

Orange Sunshine Cake

Fruit Savarins

1 package Duncan Hines® Moist Deluxe
    Yellow Cake Mix
1 jar (18 ounces) apricot preserves
¼ cup lemon juice

Assorted fresh and canned fruit (such as bananas, mandarin oranges, kiwi, strawberries, blueberries or raspberries)

1. Preheat oven to 350°F. Grease and flour 17×11×¾-inch pan.

2. Prepare cake following package directions. Bake at 350°F for 25 to 30 minutes or until toothpick inserted in center comes out clean. Cool in pan.

3. Cut cake into 40 pieces (8 equal cuts on 17-inch side, 5 on 11-inch side). Leave in pan.

4. Combine preserves and lemon juice in small saucepan. Heat on low heat until preserves are melted. Cool slightly.

5. Place fruit slices on top of each cake piece. (For a festive presentation, alternate assortment.) Place preserves in sieve above fruit. Press through to lightly coat fruit. Refrigerate until ready to serve.

■ *Tip: If you're not serving all of the cake on the same day, decorate with canned fruits because they will keep better.*

Fresh Fruit Boston Cream Pie

12 to 16 servings

1 package Duncan Hines® Moist Deluxe
    Swiss Chocolate Cake Mix
1 package (4-serving size) vanilla
    pudding and pie filling mix
    (not instant)
1½ cups milk

½ cup apricot preserves
1 tablespoon lemon juice
    Assorted fresh fruit (such as bananas, peaches, kiwi, blueberries or strawberries)

1. Preheat oven to 350°F. Grease and flour two 9-inch round cake pans.

2. Prepare, bake and cool cake following package directions.

3. Cook pudding following package directions using 1½ cups milk. Place waxed paper on surface of cooked pudding. Refrigerate until cool, about 20 minutes. Heat preserves and lemon juice in small saucepan until preserves melt. Cool slightly.

4. Cut one cake layer in half horizontally. (Freeze other layer in airtight plastic bag for a quick dessert at a later time.) Place one cut layer on serving plate. Spread with cooled pudding. Place second cut layer on top.

5. Arrange sliced fruit in attractive design on top. Place preserves in sieve above fruit. Press through to lightly coat fruit. Refrigerate until ready to serve.

■ *Tip: Unfrosted cake will keep frozen in large airtight plastic bag 3 to 4 months. Frosted cake will keep 2 to 3 months.*

Fruit Savarins

Fresh Fruit Creations
68

Chocolate Cherry Cake

12 to 16 servings

1 package Duncan Hines® Moist Deluxe
    Dark Dutch Fudge Cake Mix
1 package (8 ounces) cream cheese,
    softened
½ cup butter or margarine, softened

½ teaspoon almond extract
1 pound confectioners sugar (3½ to
    4 cups)
1 cup frozen dark sweet cherries,
    thawed, chopped, and well drained

1. Preheat oven to 350°F. Grease and flour two 9-inch round cake pans.

2. Prepare, bake and cool cake following package directions.

3. Place cream cheese, butter and almond extract in large bowl. Beat at medium speed of electric mixer until smooth. Gradually add sugar, mixing well after each addition. Measure ¾ cup of cream cheese mixture. Place in small bowl. Stir in cherries.

4. Place one cake layer on serving plate. Spread with cherry mixture. Place other layer on top. Frost sides and top with plain cream cheese frosting. Garnish top with cherries, if desired. Refrigerate until ready to serve.

■ *Tip: You can use either fresh or canned dark sweet cherries in place of frozen.*

Banana Mousse Spice Cake

12 to 16 servings

1 package Duncan Hines® Moist Deluxe
    Spice Cake Mix
1 cup milk
⅔ cup sugar
1 envelope unflavored gelatin

2 eggs, beaten
2 medium-size ripe bananas
1 tablespoon lemon juice
1 cup whipping cream
    Additional bananas, for garnish

1. Preheat oven to 350°F. Grease and flour 13×9×2-inch pan.

2. Prepare, bake and cool cake following package directions.

3. Combine milk, sugar and gelatin in medium saucepan. Cook on medium heat until mixture comes to boil. Remove from heat. Slowly stir half of hot mixture into beaten eggs. Return mixture slowly to pan while stirring. Cook on low heat 1 minute, stirring constantly. Refrigerate until thickened.

4. Mash bananas in small bowl. Stir in lemon juice. Stir into gelatin mixture. Beat whipping cream until stiff in large bowl; fold into gelatin mixture. Spread over top of cooled cake. Refrigerate until ready to serve. Garnish with additional banana slices, if desired (see Tip).

■ *Tip: To prevent fresh fruit from turning brown, slice bananas, peaches, apples, nectarines and pears into a little lemon or orange juice.*

Chocolate Cherry Cake

Strawberry Celebration Cake

Makes 12 to 16 servings

1 package Duncan Hines® Moist Deluxe
    Strawberry Supreme Cake Mix
1 cup strawberry jam, divided

1 container (16 ounces) Duncan Hines®
    Cream Cheese Layer Cake Frosting
Fresh strawberries, for garnish

1. Preheat oven to 350°F. Grease and flour 10-inch tube pan.

2. Prepare, bake and cool cake following package directions. Refrigerate cake several hours for easier cutting.

3. Cut cake horizontally into three layers (see Tip). Heat strawberry jam in small saucepan. Place one cake layer on serving plate. Spread with ½ cup jam. Place second layer on top. Spread with remaining jam. Top with third layer.

4. Frost with cream cheese frosting. Garnish with sliced strawberries, if desired. Refrigerate until ready to serve.

■ *Tip: To cut evenly, measure cake with ruler. Divide into three equal layers. Mark with toothpicks. Cut through layers using toothpicks as guide.*

Fresh Fruit 'n Cream Bundt Cake

16 servings

1 package Duncan Hines® Moist Deluxe
    French Vanilla Cake Mix
1 package (4-serving size) lemon instant
    pudding and pie filling mix
5 eggs, divided
¾ cup water

¼ cup Butter Flavor Crisco®
1 cup sugar
⅓ cup Citrus Hill® Orange Juice
1½ tablespoons lemon juice
1 cup whipping cream
Mixed fresh fruit

1. Preheat oven to 350°F. Grease and flour 10-inch tube pan or Bundt® pan.

2. Combine cake mix, pudding mix, 4 eggs, water and Butter Flavor Crisco in large bowl. Beat at low speed with electric mixer until just blended. Beat at medium speed 2 minutes. Bake at 350°F for 45 to 55 minutes or until toothpick inserted in center comes out clean. Cool following package directions.

3. Beat remaining 1 egg with fork in heavy 1-quart saucepan until blended. Stir in sugar, orange juice and lemon juice. Cook on medium heat, stirring constantly, 10 minutes or until mixture just comes to boil. Remove from heat. Refrigerate until chilled, about 30 minutes.

4. Beat whipping cream until stiff in large bowl. Just before serving fold whipped cream into sauce. To serve, spoon sauce over cake slices. Garnish with fresh fruit.

■ *Tip: You can usually find a good variety of mixed fresh fruit at a salad bar.*

Strawberry Celebration Cake

Banana Cream Cake

1 package Duncan Hines® Moist Deluxe
   Banana Supreme Cake Mix
1 package (4-serving size) vanilla
   pudding and pie filling mix
   (not instant)

1½ cups milk
1 cup whipping cream
1 cup miniature marshmallows
3 medium-size ripe bananas, sliced

1. Preheat oven to 350°F. Grease and flour two 9-inch round cake pans.

2. Prepare, bake and cool cake following package directions.

3. Cook pudding following package directions using 1½ cups milk. Place waxed paper on surface of pudding. Refrigerate until cool, about 30 minutes.

4. Beat whipping cream until stiff in large bowl. Fold into cooled pudding. Fold in marshmallows and bananas.

5. Cut each cake layer in half horizontally (see Tip). Place one cut cake layer on serving plate. Spoon on one-fourth banana mixture. Spread to edges. Repeat for remaining layers saving enough for top of cake. Refrigerate until ready to serve.

■ *Tip: To cut each cake evenly, measure cake with ruler. Divide into 2 equal layers. Mark with toothpicks. Cut through layers using toothpicks as guide.*

Fruit Tarts

1 package Duncan Hines® Moist Deluxe
   French Vanilla Cake Mix
¾ cup Butter Flavor Crisco®
2 tablespoons milk
1 egg

1 package (8 ounces) cream cheese,
   softened
Assorted fresh fruit (such as bananas,
   green grapes, kiwi, pineapple tidbits,
   strawberries or peaches)

1. Combine cake mix, Butter Flavor Crisco, milk and egg in large bowl. Beat at low speed with electric mixer until ingredients are blended. Refrigerate dough 1 hour.

2. Preheat oven to 375°F. Grease baking sheets.

3. Shape dough into 1-inch balls. Bake at 375°F for 10 to 12 minutes or until lightly browned. Cool on baking sheets 1 minute. Remove to cooling rack.

4. Spread each tart with cream cheese. Cut fruit into bite-size pieces. Arrange on top of cream cheese. Serve immediately.

■ *Tip: Undecorated tarts will keep frozen in airtight container for up to 6 weeks.*

Banana Cream Cake

Deep Dish Peach Cobbler

10 to 12 servings

1 package Duncan Hines® Moist Deluxe
   Spice Cake Mix
1 cup quick-cooking oats (not instant or
   old-fashioned)
1 cup chopped walnuts
¾ cup butter or margarine, melted
6 cups peeled and sliced peaches (about
   6 large)

½ cup water
3 tablespoons brown sugar
2 tablespoons cornstarch
1 tablespoon plus 1 teaspoon lemon juice
   Whipped topping, for garnish
   Nutmeg, for garnish

1. Preheat oven to 350°F. Grease and flour 13×9×2-inch pan.

2. Combine cake mix, oats, nuts and melted butter in large bowl. Stir until well blended. Press 2½ cups mixture in bottom of pan. Set aside remaining mixture.

3. Combine peaches, water and brown sugar in large saucepan. Simmer on low heat 5 minutes, stirring occasionally. Combine cornstarch and lemon juice in cup. Gradually add to peaches. Stir until thickened. Pour over crust. Sprinkle reserved crumbs evenly over peaches. Bake at 350°F for 25 to 30 minutes or until topping is lightly browned. Serve with whipped topping sprinkled with nutmeg, if desired.

■ *Tip: Also great served with ice cream.*

Angel Strawberry Bavarian

12 to 16 servings

1 package Duncan Hines® Angel Food
   Cake Mix
1 package (10 ounces) frozen sliced
   strawberries, thawed
1 package (4-serving size) strawberry
   flavored gelatin

1 cup boiling water
2 cups whipping cream, divided
2 tablespoons confectioners sugar
½ teaspoon vanilla extract
4 fresh strawberries

1. Preheat oven to 375°F.

2. Prepare, bake and cool cake following package directions. Cut cooled cake into 1-inch cubes.

3. Drain strawberries, reserving juice. Combine gelatin and boiling water in small bowl. Stir until gelatin is dissolved. Add enough water to strawberry juice to measure 1 cup. Add to gelatin. Refrigerate until gelatin is slightly thickened, about 30 minutes. Beat gelatin until foamy.

4. Beat 1 cup whipping cream until stiff in large bowl. Fold into gelatin along with strawberries. Alternate layers of cake cubes and strawberry mixture in 10-inch tube pan. Cover. Refrigerate overnight.

5. Unmold cake onto serving plate. Beat remaining 1 cup whipping cream, sugar and vanilla extract until stiff in large bowl. Frost cake with whipped cream mixture. Garnish with strawberries. Refrigerate until ready to serve.

■ *Tip: To beat cream quickly and assure a good texture, chill bowl and beaters before whipping cream.*

Deep Dish Peach Cobbler

Nectarine Almond Shortcake

12 servings

CAKE

½ cup slivered almonds, toasted (see Tip)

1 package Duncan Hines® Moist Deluxe Lemon Supreme Cake Mix

ALMOND WHIPPED CREAM

1 cup whipping cream
2 tablespoons confectioners sugar

½ teaspoon almond extract

FRUIT

3 cups sliced fresh nectarines
Additional nectarine slices, for garnish

Additional whipped cream, for garnish

1. Preheat oven to 350°F. Grease and flour one 9-inch round cake pan. Line another 9-inch round cake pan with aluminum foil; grease and flour aluminum foil. Spread almonds in foil-lined pan.

2. Prepare, bake and cool cake following package directions for original recipe. Remove foil carefully from almond layer.

3. **For almond whipped cream**, beat whipping cream, confectioners sugar and almond extract until stiff in large bowl.

4. To assemble cake, spread plain cake layer with whipped cream and sliced nectarines. Place almond cake layer on top. Refrigerate until ready to serve. Garnish with additional nectarine slices and whipped cream, if desired.

■ *Tip: To toast slivered almonds, spread nuts in shallow baking pan. Bake at 350°F for about 5 minutes or until golden. (Watch closely as they burn quickly.) Stir occasionally for even browning.*

Nectarine Almond Shortcake

Fruit and Yogurt Topped Cake

12 servings

1 package Duncan Hines® Moist Deluxe
   White Cake Mix
2 containers (8 ounces each) low-fat fruit
   yogurt, any flavor

Fresh fruit (same fruit as yogurt)

1. Preheat oven to 350°F. Grease and flour 13×9×2-inch pan.

2. Prepare, bake and cool cake following package directions.

3. To serve, cut cake into 3-inch squares. Place on serving plates. Spoon yogurt over each serving. Top with fresh fruit.

■ *Tip: When baking cakes, it's best not to open the oven door while the cake is baking. The sudden rush of cooler air can cause the cake to fall.*

Dump Cake

12 to 16 servings

1 can (20 ounces) crushed pineapple,
   undrained
1 can (21 ounces) cherry pie filling
1 package Duncan Hines® Moist Deluxe
   Yellow Cake Mix

1 cup chopped pecans or walnuts
½ cup butter or margarine, cut into thin
   slices

1. Preheat oven to 350°F. Grease 13×9×2-inch pan.

2. Dump undrained pineapple into pan. Spread evenly. Dump in pie filling. Spread evenly. Sprinkle cake mix evenly over cherry layer. Sprinkle pecans over cake mix. Dot with butter. Bake at 350°F for 50 minutes or until top is lightly browned. Serve warm or at room temperature.

■ *Tip: You can use Duncan Hines® Moist Deluxe Pineapple Supreme Cake Mix in place of Yellow Cake Mix.*

Fruit and Yogurt Topped Cake

Cherry Filled Chocolate Cake

12 to 16 servings

1 package Duncan Hines® Moist Deluxe
   Devil's Food Cake Mix
2 envelopes whipped topping mix
1 package (4-serving size) chocolate
   instant pudding and pie filling mix

1¼ cups milk
¼ teaspoon almond extract
1 can (21 ounces) light cherry pie filling,
   divided

1. Preheat oven to 350°F. Grease and flour two 9-inch round cake pans.

2. Prepare, bake and cool cake following package directions.

3. Combine topping mix, pudding mix, milk and almond extract in medium bowl. Beat at medium speed with electric mixer until stiff, about 3 minutes.

4. To assemble, place one cake layer on serving plate. Make a 1-inch wide by ½-inch high ring of chocolate mixture around top edge of cake.

5. Reserve ¾ cup of cherry filling. Spoon remaining filling in center of cake. Spread to edge of chocolate ring. Place second cake layer on top. Spoon reserved cherries in center; spread into a circle.

6. Frost sides of cake and over top edge to ring of cherries with remaining chocolate mixture. Refrigerate at least 1 hour before serving. Store leftovers in refrigerator.

■ *Tip: You can use other fruit pie filling or other flavors pudding mix in place of the cherry pie filling and chocolate pudding.*

Peach Chantilly

12 servings

1 package Duncan Hines® Moist Deluxe
   White Cake Mix
2 containers (8 ounces each) peach
   yogurt

1 cup frozen non-dairy whipped topping,
   thawed
2 peaches
   Nutmeg

1. Preheat oven to 350°F. Grease and flour 13×9×2-inch pan.

2. Prepare, bake and cool cake following package directions.

3. Place yogurt in small bowl. Fold in whipped topping. Finely dice 1 peach; fold into topping. Cut second peach into 12 thin slices.

4. To serve, cut cake into 3-inch squares. Place on serving plates. Spoon topping on each serving; top with peach slice. Sprinkle with nutmeg.

■ *Tip: You can use other yogurt flavors and fresh fruit in place of peach yogurt and peaches.*

Pineapple Cream Supreme

16 servings

1 package Duncan Hines® Moist Deluxe
   Pineapple Supreme Cake Mix
1 package (8 ounces) cream cheese,
   softened
2 tablespoons milk

1 package (4-serving size) vanilla instant
   pudding and pie filling mix
1 can (8 ounces) crushed pineapple,
   undrained
1½ cups fresh blueberries, optional

1. Preheat oven to 350°F. Grease and flour 13×9×2-inch pan.

2. Prepare, bake and cool cake following package directions.

3. Beat cream cheese in small bowl at medium speed with electric mixer until smooth. Add milk; beat until creamy. Add pudding mix; beat until mixed. Add pineapple; beat 1 minute. Fold in blueberries by hand. Spread over top of cooled cake. Refrigerate until ready to serve.

■ *Tip: To keep the cake's fresh flavor, tent aluminum foil over top of pan and seal edges tightly.*

Fruit Cocktail Cake

12 servings

1 package Duncan Hines® Moist Deluxe
   Yellow Cake Mix
1 package (4-serving size) lemon instant
   pudding and pie filling mix
4 eggs
1 can (16 ounces) fruit cocktail,
   undrained

1 cup flaked coconut
¼ cup Crisco® Oil or Puritan® Oil
¼ cup quartered maraschino cherries
½ cup chopped walnuts

1. Preheat oven to 350°F. Grease and flour 13×9×2-inch pan.

2. Combine cake mix, pudding mix, eggs, fruit cocktail, coconut, oil and cherries in large bowl. Beat at medium speed with electric mixer for 4 minutes. Pour into pan. Sprinkle top with walnuts. Bake at 350°F for 45 to 50 minutes or until toothpick inserted in center comes out clean. Cool in pan. Cut into 3-inch squares.

■ *Tip: You can use Duncan Hines® Moist Deluxe Pineapple Supreme or Moist Deluxe Banana Supreme Cake mix in place of Yellow Cake Mix.*

Carousel Cake

12 to 16 servings

1 package Duncan Hines® Moist Deluxe
   Cake Mix (any flavor)
1 container (16 ounces) Duncan Hines®
   Vanilla or Cream Cheese Layer Cake
   Frosting

Assorted garnishes such as chopped
nuts, toasted coconut, mini chocolate
chips, peanut butter chips, jelly
beans, slivered almonds, chocolate
decors or colored decors

1. Preheat oven to 350°F. Grease and flour two 9-inch round cake pans.

2. Prepare, bake and cool cake following package directions.

3. Frost cake with vanilla frosting. Score top of cake into 8 equal wedges. Top each wedge with a different garnish of your choice.

■ *Tip: Change decorations for seasonal or party themes.*

Black Eyed Susan Cake

12 to 16 servings

1 package Duncan Hines® Moist Deluxe
   Fudge Marble Cake Mix
1 container (16 ounces) Duncan Hines®
   Chocolate Layer Cake Frosting

1 container (16 ounces) Duncan Hines®
   Lemon Layer Cake Frosting

1. Preheat oven to 350°F. Grease and flour two 9-inch round cake pans.

2. Prepare, bake and cool cake following package directions.

3. Place one cake layer on serving plate. Frost with chocolate frosting to within ¼ inch of edge. Place second layer on top. Frost top with chocolate frosting to within 1½ inches of edge.

4. Frost sides and top edge with lemon frosting. Use knife to pull out and swirl frosting on top to decorate.

■ *Tip: For a delicious snack, spread leftover frosting between vanilla wafers.*

Carousel Cake

Clown Cupcakes

12 clown cupcakes

1 package Duncan Hines® Moist Deluxe
   Yellow Cake Mix
12 scoops vanilla ice cream
1 package (12 count) sugar ice cream
   cones

1 container (7 ounces) refrigerated
   aerosol whipped cream
Assorted colored decors
Assorted candies for eyes, nose and
   mouth

1. Preheat oven to 350°F. Place 2½-inch paper liners in 24 muffin cups.

2. Prepare, bake and cool cupcakes following package directions.

3. To assemble each clown, remove paper from cupcake. Place top-side down on serving plate. Top with a scoop of ice cream. Place cone on ice cream for hat. Spray whipped cream around bottom of cupcake for collar. Spray three small dots up front of cone. Sprinkle whipped cream with assorted colored decors. Use candies to make clown's face.

Note: This recipe makes 24 cupcakes: 12 to make into "clowns" and 12 to freeze for later use. Cupcakes will keep frozen in airtight container for up to 6 weeks.

■ *Tip: For easier preparation, make the ice cream balls ahead of time. Scoop out balls of ice cream, place on baking sheet or in bowl and return to freezer to firm.*

Polka-Dot Cookies

4 dozen cookies

1 package Duncan Hines® Moist Deluxe
   Yellow Cake Mix
¾ cup Butter Flavor Crisco®

2 eggs, separated
1 tablespoon milk
Assorted colored decors

1. Preheat oven to 375°F. Grease baking sheets.

2. Combine cake mix, Butter Flavor Crisco, egg yolks and milk in large bowl. Shape into 1-inch balls.

3. Beat egg whites slightly in small bowl. Dip balls into egg whites. Roll in assorted colored decors. Bake at 375°F for 8 to 10 minutes or until lightly browned. Cool on baking sheet 1 minute. Remove to cooling rack.

■ *Tip: You can frost cookies with any flavor Duncan Hines® frosting instead of rolling cookies in assorted colored decors.*

Clown Cupcakes

Ice Cream Cookie Sandwich

10 to 12 servings

2 pints chocolate chip ice cream, softened
1 package Duncan Hines® Moist Deluxe Dark Dutch Fudge Cake Mix

½ cup butter or margarine, softened

1. Line bottom of one 9-inch round cake pan with aluminum foil. Spread ice cream in pan. Return to freezer until firm. Run knife around edge of pan to loosen ice cream. Remove from pan. Wrap in foil and return to freezer.

2. Preheat oven to 350°F. Line bottom of two 9-inch round cake pans with aluminum foil. Place cake mix in large bowl. Add butter. Mix until crumbs form. Place half the cake mix in each pan. Press lightly. Bake at 350°F for 15 minutes or until browned around edges; do not overbake. Cool 10 minutes. Remove from pans. Remove foil from cookie layers. Cool completely.

3. To assemble, place one cookie layer on serving plate. Top with ice cream. Peel off foil. Place second cookie layer on top. Wrap in foil and freeze 2 hours. To keep longer, store in airtight container.

■ *Tip: You can use lemon sherbet and Duncan Hines® Moist Deluxe Lemon Supreme Cake Mix in place of chocolate chip ice cream and Moist Deluxe Dark Dutch Fudge Cake Mix.*

Dessert Pizza Pies

24 servings

1 package Duncan Hines® Moist Deluxe Yellow Cake Mix
1 egg
½ cup butter or margarine
2 packages (8 ounces each) cream cheese, softened

½ cup confectioners sugar
1½ cups strawberry jam
½ cup candy coated chocolate pieces
1 ounce white chocolate, shaved

1. Preheat oven to 350°F. Grease 10-inch circle on 2 baking sheets.

2. For crust, combine cake mix, egg and butter in large bowl. Beat at low speed with electric mixer until blended. Place half the mixture in center of each greased circle. Press evenly to edge of circle. Bake at 350°F for 15 minutes or until lightly browned. Cool on baking sheets.

3. For topping, combine cream cheese and confectioners sugar in small bowl. Beat at low speed with electric mixer until smooth. Spread over cooled circles. Spread ¾ cup strawberry jam on top of cream cheese layer. Decorate each with ¼ cup chocolate pieces. Sprinkle with shaved white chocolate. Cut each circle into 12 servings.

■ *Tip: You can use any candy pieces in place of chocolate pieces.*

Ice Cream Cookie Sandwich

Banana Split Refrigerator Cake

12 servings

1 package Duncan Hines® Moist Deluxe
   Banana Supreme Cake Mix
1 envelope whipped topping mix
1 package (4-serving size) vanilla instant
   pudding and pie filling mix
1½ cups milk
1 teaspoon vanilla extract
6 maraschino cherries, drained and
   halved

1 medium-size ripe banana, sliced
½ cup thinly sliced fresh pineapple pieces
¼ cup coarsely chopped pecans or
   walnuts
½ cup hot fudge ice cream topping,
   warmed

1. Preheat oven to 350°F. Grease and flour 13×9×2-inch pan.

2. Prepare, bake and cool cake following package directions.

3. Combine topping mix, pudding mix, milk and vanilla extract in large bowl. Beat at medium speed with electric mixer until stiff. Spread over cooled cake. Place maraschino cherry halves, banana slices, pineapple pieces and chopped pecans randomly on topping. Drizzle with fudge topping. Refrigerate until ready to serve. Cut into 3-inch squares.

■ *Tip: To prevent banana slices from darkening, slice into small amount diluted lemon juice. Drain thoroughly before placing on cake.*

Butterfly Cake

12 to 16 servings

1 package Duncan Hines® Moist Deluxe
   Yellow or Lemon Supreme Cake Mix
2 containers (16 ounces) Duncan Hines®
   Vanilla or Cream Cheese Layer Cake
   Frosting, divided

Red food coloring
Red licorice laces
Pastel candy wafers

1. Preheat oven to 350°F. Grease and flour two 9-inch round cake pans.

2. Prepare, bake and cool cake following package directions.

3. Fill and frost with vanilla frosting as for 2 layer cake. Refrigerate cake 1 hour for easier handling. Place remaining frosting in small bowl. Add a few drops red food coloring to tint frosting pink.

4. To assemble, cut cake in half. Place on serving plate with round sides touching and with cut sides out. Outline with pink frosting using decorator's tube (see Note). Arrange 2 licorice laces for feelers. Decorate with candy wafers for spots.

Note: If decorator's tube is not available, place tinted frosting in small airtight plastic bag. Seal top and cut off a tiny bottom corner to use as tip.

■ *Tip: Leftover cake will keep frozen in airtight container for up to 6 weeks.*

Banana Split Refrigerator Cake

Rainbow Cupcakes

24 cupcakes

CAKE

1 package Duncan Hines® Moist Deluxe
    Fudge Marble Cake Mix

Red and green food coloring

FROSTING

1 pound confectioners sugar (3½ to
    4 cups)
½ cup Butter Flavor Crisco®
⅓ cup milk

1 teaspoon vanilla extract
2 tablespoons cocoa
Red and green food coloring
Assorted colored decors

1. Preheat oven to 350°F. Place 2½-inch paper liners in 24 muffin cups.

2. **For cake**, set aside cocoa packet. Prepare cake mix following package directions. Divide batter into thirds and place in 3 different bowls. Stir cocoa packet into one. Add 5 drops red food coloring to another. Add 5 drops green food coloring to the third. Stir each just until blended.

3. Layer 1 tablespoon of each color batter into each muffin cup. Bake at 350°F for 20 to 25 minutes. Cool completely.

4. **For frosting**, combine sugar, Butter Flavor Crisco, milk and vanilla extract in medium bowl. Beat at low speed with electric mixer until blended. Scrape bowl. Beat at high speed for 2 minutes.

5. Divide frosting into thirds and place in 3 different bowls. Add cocoa to one. Add a few drops red food coloring to another. Add a few drops green food coloring to the third. Stir each until well blended. Frost cupcakes with a small amount of each color frosting. Sprinkle with assorted colored decors.

■ *Tip: An easy way to fill muffin cups is to place the batter in a 2- or 4-cup glass measure. Pour desired amount of batter into each muffin cup. Use a spatula to stop the flow of batter.*

Rainbow Cupcakes